Heart's Cry
Poetry For The Soul

Cynthia Haynes

© 2012 by Cynthia Haynes. All rights reserved.

This book or parts thereof may not be reproduced in any form, stored in a retrieval system, or transmitted in any form by any means – electronic, mechanical, photocopy, recording, or otherwise – without prior written permission of the author, except as provided by United States copyright law.

Unless otherwise quoted, all Scripture quotations are from the Holy Bible, New King James Version, (NKJV). Copyright © 1979 1980 1982. Thomas Nelson, Inc. Used by permission all rights reserved.

Scriptures marked (KJV) are taken from the Holy Bible, King James Version.

Published by: Cynthia Haynes
Artisticoverflow.com
Printed in the U.S.A.

ISBN-13: 978-0-9969430-0-0
ISBN-10: 0996943005
Library of Congress Control Number: 2015919805

Dedication

This book is dedicated to my husband; thank you for your support and for always standing by me. And to my children; never give up on your dreams for with God all things are possible.

Table of Contents

Introduction	1
Potter	3
Free Me	5
Divine Revelation	8
No Evil	11
Asked Why	13
My plea	15
The Battle	17
Stand	20
I Had a Talk with God	22
Lies	26
Save Me	29
Purgatory	31
Purgatory Pt. 2	34

Purgatory Pt. 3 37

Father, Can You Hear Me? 40

Messenger of God 43

The Keys to My Deliverance 46

To Touch the Hem of His Garment 51

God's Gonna Trouble the Water 59

This Too Shall Pass 70

Flowin' with God 76

Don't get it Twisted (I Know Who I Am) 86

Introduction

Walking the path to faith can be very personal and confusing. Although I always had spirituality, I had to go through many trials and tribulations before building my personal relationship with the Lord and wholly accepting Him as the center of my life. On my way, I fell multiple times and made mistakes that I thought were irreparable. These things, however, made me stronger and helped me on my spiritual journey to become a true woman of God; for Him, for myself, for my children, for my husband and for other people I came across along the way.

Heart's Cry is very special to my heart, and was written with the hope that the words within would reach the people in need of them most and even those who are unaware that they need them. As God has shown us time and time again, He puts people in our paths to help us see the things that we could or would not normally see. As children of God, we are all free to make choices; we can either be righteous or unrighteous. In some cases, our enemies test our faith by setting evil and temptation before us. When you come across a situation where these obstacles are placed in your path to hinder and discourage you, simply let go and let God, for He is "faithful and just to forgive our sins, and to cleanse us from all unrighteousness" (1 John 1:9).

We have all gone through struggles or situations that have made us question God or feel abandoned. However, I pray that these poems will uplift and encourage you, so that deep within your heart you understand and remember that there is nothing that God cannot solve. Despite our doubts, troubles, misfortunes and suffering, God can and does bring healing and peace to those who walk by faith. As Proverbs 3:5-6 encourages us "Trust in the LORD with all thine heart; and lean not unto thine own understanding. In all thy ways acknowledge him, and he shall direct thy paths."

These words written in *Heart's Cry* are my testimony, and I share it with all of you with the hope that you may be comforted—reassured—enriched. God bless you always.

Cynthia Haynes

Isaiah 64:8

"But now, O LORD, thou art our father; we are the clay, and thou our potter; and we all are the work of thy hand."

Potter

The master potter

Are you molding me?

I am but a pile of clay waiting to be molded

Your pupil

Waiting to be taught

Your servant

Waiting to serve

I hunger and thirst for righteousness

Fill me

No longer do I wish to eat bitter fruit

Obedience

Cynthia Haynes

I am ready to be an obedient child

Temptation

Give me the strength to fight the enemy

Weakness

Give me wisdom to prevail over evil doers

I will be humble

Never losing my faith

I can stand tall

For now I am walking with the Lord.

2 Corinthians 3:17

"Now the Lord is that Spirit: and where the Spirit of the Lord is, there is liberty".

Free Me

You have led me out of treacherous waters.

I was drowning in pity.

Suffocating in pain.

I was trapped in a bottomless pit reaching out.

My soul was crying.

Free Me! Free Me!

My mind saying I can get through this.

My spirit says only with God can you make it.

The sadness rings in my ears.

The pain echoes in my soul.

I close my eyes, complete darkness—into a deep sleep I go.

Visions of the past, mistakes I've made, sadness I've experienced, pain I've suffered haunts me.

Tears begin to roll out of my eyes, one by one.

Tears that I have held in.

Each signifying a loss, a deep sorrow, turmoil.

More tears begin to come.

I am alone!

The heartache is so overwhelming; it feels as if a knife has pierced my heart.

I am alone!

It is quiet, calmness comes over me.

A warm gentle feeling runs through my body.

I am not alone; he has been with me the whole time.

Holding me when things were unbearable.

Loving me when I felt unloved.

Never forgetting me, even when I had forgotten him.

Tears start to come again; only this time tears of joy.

He loves me.

God really loves me.

God heard my soul crying,

Free Me! Free me!

God has freed me.

I AM FREE!

This poem was written several years ago. No one is born saved and we can either make the walk with God easy or hard. I knew of God and I wanted a relationship with Him, but I also wanted the love of a man. So, I put the love of a man before God. I expected God to maintain my relationship, but it was wrong in His sight. When problems started in my relationship with the man in my life, I blamed God. Then one day he spoke to me as I wrote this poem, and he revealed to me what the real problem was—he gave me a Divine revelation.

2 Corinthians 4:6 NKJV

"For it is the God who commanded light to shine out of darkness, who has shone in our hearts to give the light of the knowledge of the glory of God in the face of Jesus Christ."

Divine Revelation

I have seen the light, but I choose darkness

I know wrong from right, but I choose to do wrong

By doing wrong

Indulging in sin

Forgetting the truth

I have inflicted pain upon myself.

How can I expect you to be in the midst of corruption and evildoing?

How could you protect me when I abandoned you?

I blame you for the pain I am in

But it is of my own doing

I choose death over life

Pain over joy

Confusion over peace

My spirit hungers and thirsts

Because I'd rather participate in fornication

Instead of feeding my spirit

How can you bless me

When I am of the world

And live in corruption and sin?

I choose the love of a man

Cynthia Haynes

Instead of you and your love

How can my relationship be prosperous?

When it is wrong and goes against you

I shall never find peace

Until I find you…

Psalm 23:4 NKJV

"Yea, though I walk through the valley of the shadow of death
I will fear no evil;
For You are with me;
Your rod and You staff, they comfort me."

No Evil

I will fear no evil

The spirit of God is with me

The enemy has no power over me

God has made me whole

The world and the wicked can't entice

The Lord has strengthened me

Sin won't stop me

The Savior is here with me

Temptation won't weaken me

Cynthia Haynes

The Almighty will carry me

I will not lose focus

The Lord is guiding me.

1 John 4:19 NKJV

"We love Him because He first loved us."

Asked Why

I asked God why.

Why do you let me go through pain and suffering?

He said, *you create the pain and suffering, not Me.*

I will console you if you let Me.

God asked me, *Where has your faith gone?*

It was there when all was well, but when the trials began you doubted Me.

As if you never had faith.

I asked God why He left me in my time of despair.

I did not leave you. I am here as I have always been.

You started to do things on your own and began to question Me.

God, why when I was drowning in sadness, reaching out my hand

Why didn't you take it?

I did take your hand, but you would rather drown than receive help from anyone, including Me.

Well, God, why won't you forgive me?

I have forgiven you; it is you who would not forgive yourself.

Why don't you love me?

I do love you, my child; it is you who does not love Me.

God, what am I fighting for?

Me. You are fighting for me.

Isaiah 41:10 NKJV

"Fear not, for I am with you;
Be not dismayed, for I am your God.
I will strengthen you,
Yes, I will help you,
I will uphold you with My righteous right hand."

My plea

I am broken; fix me

I am lost; find me

My mind is corrupt; mold me into a righteous person

My heart is wounded; heal me

My soul is in pain

Doubt fills my head

Sorrow runs through me

Set me free

Cynthia Haynes

I need comfort; comfort me

I need strength; strengthen me

Reconstruct me and make me whole.

Ephesians 6:12

"For we wrestle not against flesh and blood, but against principalities, against powers, against the rulers of darkness of this world, against spiritual wickedness in high places."

Letting go and letting God take over is what it is all about. I have tried to do many things on my own and have fallen every time. The spiritual warfare that goes on constantly is real.

When I wrote this I could literally feel the pull between my flesh and my spirit. Although I felt like giving up, God sent a remarkable servant of his to encourage me to push through. I thank God for sending someone my way to enable me to pick myself up and to put on the armor of God. What an awesome God we serve.

The Battle

The battle between good and evil, life and death

My flesh pulling me in one direction, my spirit in another

The enemy trying to steal my joy, my soul

Cynthia Haynes

Trying to make it back to my Father

Trying to be a worthy and loyal soldier

Fierce shots made to my mind, blows made to my heart

Attacks on my flesh

Wounded and my spirit weary

Almost to my knees

Ready to throw my hands up in defeat

An angelic warrior whispers to me

"Push through it, push your way through"

Courage to now go on, regaining my strength

Now wearing the Lord's armor, ready to fight in the war

Marching through the storm, singing through the fire

My friends lost in the destruction

Loved ones too injured to go on

Soldiers in distress

The enemy still trying to slay me

Marching still, victory so close

Freedom!

Freer with each step I take

The adversary confused, no more weapons to use

The enemy defeated

Conquering the obstacles

Resisting evil

Standing against the enemy

Marching through the pain

Letting go and letting God.

1 Corinthians 16:13 NKJV

"*Watch, stand fast in the faith, be brave, be strong.*"

Stand

Through the struggle and time of despair

My faith will not be shaken and I will stand

Through the lies and deceit of the world

The fiery darts of the enemy

Through the battle, the battle between my flesh and my spirit

I will stand

Any obstacle thrown before me

I shall not fall

I will stand

Through the trials and tribulations

Sorrow and pain

Through my darkest hours

I will not be broken

I will stand

Through the temptation

Ridicule and persecution

Through the wickedness of the world

Fire and rain

I will stand

I stand not in my own strength

But in the strength of the Lord

No matter what comes my way

I will stand.

Deuteronomy 31:8 NKJV

"And the Lord, He is the One who goes before you. He will be with you; He will not leave you nor forsake you; do not fear nor be dismayed."

I Had a Talk with God

I had a talk with God today
As I sat in silence
So many things rushing through my mind
He came to me

Child, what troubles you?

Father, so many days I forget you
I do what I want even though it is wrong

Child haven't you learned by now?
No matter what you do, I will never leave nor forsake you

Father, I have walked away time and time again

Child
I will come and get you; you belong to me
And to my flock

Father, some days my past comes to haunt me
And I hate the reflection I see

My precious child
That is the enemy trying to take you away from me
But all that was taken care of at Calvary

Father, I don't understand why
I have gone through so much pain and suffering

My child, it is not always for you to understand
But know this—it is all part of my divine plan

Father, I have experienced so much darkness
Gone astray and at times I don't even pray

My beloved child, it is the darkness that brings you to the light
Even if you go astray, child, you must always pray

Cynthia Haynes

Father, at times I feel like giving up
I feel like I have no strength to go on

My child, you must walk in my strength
Not in your own

This is why things have gone so very wrong

Father
Sometimes I get so weak and won't swallow my pride
And say, "Please. Please Daddy, come help me!"

Ah, child
Here is the key—on your knees you humble yourself before me
All you have to do is believe

Believe I can heal any affliction, sickness or disease...

No matter what you have been through
What you will go through
I WILL NEVER LEAVE YOUR SIDE
You must never lose faith

Father, this walk is so hard

My daughter, it is as hard as you make it
Through me, you can do all things

Just remember, my precious child
No matter what lies the enemy tells
Or what will arise
You have victory because I am on your side
Remember to love me
For I first loved you
And one day I will say
"This is my beloved child... with whom I am well pleased..."

John 10:10

"The thief does not come except to steal, and to kill, and to destroy. I have come that they may have life, and that they may have it more abundantly."

Lies

God is calling me back
The enemy reminding me of what I lack

Telling me I am not free
I wish Satan would just let me be

Always talking in my ear
So I won't be able to hear

Hear my Father's voice
Satan is lying to me, saying I don't have a choice

Reminding me I am a sinner
Whispering you will never be a winner

My soul screams
Go back to the only one who redeems

Attempting to control my mind
Wanting to keep me blind

I must be brave
No longer can I be a slave

I'm tired of these chains
How could I forget my GOD reigns?

Need to make God the head of my life
Then, and only then, will my heart not feel strife

So Father, I ask you to purify me
Father, set me free

Free me from all this bondage
Then there may be no more blockage

I desire to be selfless
So I can experience holiness

Cynthia Haynes

Faith is what I long for
I don't want to get lost in the war

Father, as I pray
I pray I stop going astray

I pray you give me wisdom
Don't want to be a victim

Greater is He that is in me
I know my God will set me free.

2 Corinthians 1:10

"Who delivered us from so great a death, and does deliver us; in whom we trust that He will still deliver us"

Save Me

Time to get back in the race

All of my pain and fears I must face

My soul longs to feel your spiritual embrace

I must get back to my Father

My soul can't take this any longer

I cry out to you

'Cause I know nothing else to do

I have not ceased to your call

I know now this is why I fall

Fall deeper into despair

But I know that you can repair

Cynthia Haynes

Repair my wounded heart

Now it's time for a new start

The world has tried to break me

Lord, come and save me.

2 Corinthians 10:4 NKJV

"For the weapons of our warfare are not carnal but mighty in God for pulling down strongholds"

Purgatory

I have walked away

Conflicted within myself

My vision blurry

My mind colliding with my heart

Spirit contesting my flesh

Being pulled in various directions

The confusion intensifies with each passing day

My faith has faltered

Doubt now runs through me

Grief penetrating the very depths of my soul

Anger coursing through my veins

Cynthia Haynes

Each day a new battle

I AM PARALYZED

Will the suffering end?

Entangled in my wants

Kept in bondage by my selfishness

The course unknown to me

Hate enslaves me

Your presence I can no longer feel

I cannot find my way back

A part of me does not want to

Grown accustomed to the sorrow

Cruelty has hardened me

Disappointment has molded me

My spirit screaming

FEED ME!!

Mingling with temptation

Viewing things on an intellectual level

Not allowing God to fit in the equation

Miserable and stubborn

Almost unable to stand

Consumed with disbelief

Emotions running rapid

It… has…begun

The combat for my life

The war for my soul

Purgatory Pt. 2

~Warfare~

The trap set in motion

Feeling forsaken

My mind chaotic

Emotionally drained

Spiritual anorexia

Demons of the past coming to haunt me

My soul a wreck

Ravaged by inner turmoil

My psyche in an uproar

God calling me back

Resentful for the suffering

My heart inflamed with pain

My soul won't be still

Chastised for my sins

My mind a playground for wretchedness

Fixated on "an eye for an eye"

Unable to do warfare

Lacerations made to my heart

Afflicted and staggering

In distress

Lack of will power

Lasciviousness replacing righteousness

Inside about to erupt

Overtaken by anguish

My spirit wailing

I am enraged

Angry

Feeling I am being punished

Emotional hell

Riots all around

Compromising my character

Cynthia Haynes

Helpless to the attacks

Powerless in battle

Naked with no armor

My spirit is losing

The flesh is overpowering

Taking over

My spirit is wounded

It is broken

Purgatory Pt. 3

~The Final Chapter~

My spirit is broken

To my knees in defeat

The enemy pleased

I see a shining light

The heaviness in my heart taken away

My soul replenished

God lifting me up

Up out of hell

Standing by my side

As I do warfare

Restoring my spirit

I march ahead

Cynthia Haynes

The word still in me

"No weapon formed against me shall prosper"

My spiritual armor back on

Loins girt about with truth

Breastplate of righteousness

Feet shod with the preparation of the gospel of peace

Taking the shield of faith

The helmet of salvation

The sword of the Spirit

Cutting the chains

Chains that bind me

Demons of my past

Cast into the pit of hell

Anger replaced with JOY

Trading hate for LOVE

Selfishness for selflessness

No longer paralyzed

Able to move forward

Abide in the flesh no more

His greatness manifested

Freed from slavery

Dying to self

I am still

Peace fills me

God's beauty all around me

I feel serenity

My spirit rejoicing

Angels celebrating

I cry

No more shackles

I have victory!

No more veil of darkness over me

I am precious in the sight of the Lord

His Love, Everlasting…

Psalm 107:28-29 NKJV

28 *"Then they cry out to the* LORD IN THEIR TROUBLE,
And He brings them out of their distresses.

*29 He calms the storm,
So that its waves are still."*

Father, Can You Hear Me?

Father, can you hear me?

Can you hear my silent tears?

The sadness rushing through me like a river

A whirlwind of confusion running through me

Father, can you hear me?

The winds furiously coming, trying to destroy everything in its path

The storm violently tearing down what's in its way

As a tornado comes and sucks everything up, so has the truth been sucked away

Father, can you hear me?

As a desert is dry, so is my spirit

I have not had food or drink as if I've been wandering in the wilderness for years

Wandering in darkness, I cannot see the light

Father, can you hear me?

I have lost my sight, as though I was born blind

Flooding in the rapid waters of my sins

Consumed by the feeling of failure

I have disappointed my Father so

The choices I have made will be my destruction

Father, can you hear me?

The unspoken words I say every day

Come swiftly and bring me back

Come quick as a hurricane and cleanse me

As an earthquake, come and abolish my ungodly ways

As before a storm, come calm my spirit

Cynthia Haynes

Father, can you hear me?

Come in, come dwell here again

Come quickly

Father, can you hear me?

This poem is dedicated to Pastor Tammy.

Messenger of God

Who is this woman?

This Pastor

She is a woman of valor

She carries a badge of honor

Waving her flag of victory

Her flag bearing two colors

Red for the blood

Of her crucifixion

Dying to the flesh daily

And white

For the pureness of heart

Who is this woman?

This woman who speaks wisdom

Cynthia Haynes

She is obedient

A vessel

An instrument

Dedicated to the Lord

A soldier in His army

A prayer warrior

Prayer and supplication is her food

The Lord is her portion

Who is this woman?

This prophet

When she opens her mouth

She blesses many

God, the Father

Gets the Glory

The devil trembles

She allows God to use her

To touch other's lives

To give revelation to the lost

Those in need

Who is this woman?

She has the strength of a thousand men

More knowledge

Than any scholar

She has faith to move mountains

And more weapons

Than any army

Who is this woman?

This servant

The Glory of the Lord is upon her

His fire rains on her

This one

Sent by God

Molded in His hands

Who is this woman?

She is a messenger of God

Psalm 34:17 NKJV

*"The righteous cry out, and the L*ORD HEARS,
And delivers them out of all their troubles."

The Keys to My Deliverance

Don't want to hurt anymore

A child of God

Yes

A servant of God

No

The deposits made in my soul

Have me bound to my emotions

Saying I want to be free

But I won't go before Him

With a right heart

Still holding on to the past

All of the pain

My mind

Spirit

Body

And soul

Not in one accord

Prayer changes things

But afraid of the change

A part of me is dying to be free

The other part held captive

Being torn into

Being of a double mind

Ashamed to open my mouth

Still wondering what people will think

Won't lift my voice up to the Lord

Release my tongue

I know what to do

I move forward

And then Satan and his devices

Cynthia Haynes

I take two steps back

Having to start over

Feeling frustrated

Worthless

Trying to figure out who I am in Christ

Not knowing my authority

Satan keeps riding me

Because I am so close to my break through

Oh, how I long to be free

Yes

Who the Son sets free

Is free indeed

I have asked to be free

Or did I ask

And then took it back

CRY OUT TO ME!

I keep hearing

CRY OUT TO ME!!

The devil still playing me like a fiddle

Keep going back to the water

What a fool I have been

Because I know the truth

The Lord has given me the keys

Yet I ask everyone else for help

When all He wants

Is for me to ask Him

So with my pen

God reveals to me

The things I need to do

Just give it to Him

The battle is His

So if I really want freedom

Real freedom

Not free today

Bound tomorrow

But true freedom

Lift my voice

And cry out to Him

Cynthia Haynes

Stop being a skeptic

A spectator

Just cry out

My deliverance

Is surely to come

Matthew 9:20- 23 KJV

And, behold, a woman, which was diseased with an issue of blood twelve years, came behind him, and touched the hem of his garment:

[21] For she said within herself, If I may but touch his garment, I shall be whole.

[22] But Jesus turned him about, and when he saw her, he said, Daughter, be of good comfort; thy faith hath made thee whole. And the woman was made whole from that hour.

To Touch the Hem of His Garment

How I long to touch the hem of His garment

I have watched as others have

And received their deliverance

Yet I still watch

But only if I could

Cynthia Haynes

Touch the hem of His garment

Even if

For a brief moment

With a touch

To bring

Healing

Deliverance

Wholeness

With just the slightest touch

And I watch

And I watch

And I watch

I keep watching

Yearning to move forward

To touch the hem of His garment

But my feet

My feet

My feet

My feet are in shackles

Lacking the strength to push

To push through the crowd

To push through the crowd

To push through the crowd

To push through

Courage fills me

The spirit of the Lord draws me

So I walk

And I push

I begin to push through the crowd

The slander

The gossip

The fear

The doubt

And I push

I push through the crowd

The sorrow

The anger

The bitterness

Cynthia Haynes

The pain

OH!!!

All of the pain

The pain

All the pain of my past

The demons trying to keep me enslaved

Yet I push

And I push

So close

To touch the hem

So close

So close

So close

And I push through the crowd

Thousands of chains needing to be broken

Pushing through

Low self esteem

Lack of self worth

Seeking to please others

Not caring

Not caring anymore

What people will say

What they think

I push harder

Running now

To touch the hem of His garment

Can't see nothing else

Don't care about anything else

To be made whole

To be whole

Is right there

Fighting to get there

Leaving others behind to get there

So I push

I push

I push through the crowd

Satan behind me

YOU CAN'T HAVE ANYMORE!

NO MORE!

Pushing through

Unforgiveness

The logic and ways of the world

Running faster now

To touch the hem of His garment

I fall

But I get up

Dirty

But I push through

Weak

But I push through

Tormented

But I push through

Wounded

But I push through

Lost

But I push through

Afflicted

But I push through

Hurt

But I push through

Beaten

But I push through

Whipped

But I push through

I stop

I am here

All I have to do

Is reach out my hand

And touch the hem of His garment

I've come too far

To go back now

So I put forth my hand

Hallelujah!

Hallelujah!

Hallelujah!

Glory be to God!

Cynthia Haynes

Truly, joy cometh

Healing

Deliverance

No more lame to the sadness

Love fills me

All because

I touched the hem of His garment.

John 5:4

"For an angel went down at a certain season into the pool, and troubled the water: whosoever then first after the troubling of the water stepped in was made whole of whatsoever disease he had."

God's Gonna Trouble the Water

Joy

Freedom

Wholeness

All unknown to me

Life has broken me down

My past coming back to haunt me

With the dawning of a new day

But still

Something in me

Cynthia Haynes

Yearns to be free

To be whole

If I can just make it to the water

I know

God's gonna trouble the water

He will make me whole

The road is far off

Something stirs in my spirit

This road

No one can take me

The world has left me numb

Empty

The yearning is still there

Not to be trapped by fear

To know the joy of the Lord

No more strongholds

Generational curses

Bitterness

Insecurity

Doubt

Self-disgust

But

To be free

To mount up with wings as eagles

Run and not be weary

Walk and not faint

My soul cries

Yes

My spirit screams

Freedom

Lies upon lies

To keep me from going to the water

Lie

After Lie

I'm not good enough

I will just fail

God can't love me

I will never make it

Cynthia Haynes

So many lies

I'm not listening

I'll make it

I'll make it there

I'm going

I don't care if my friends don't go

I don't care

If my sister and brother don't go

I don't care

If my mama and daddy don't go

I have to go

Because I need to be made whole

With so many trials, my heart has grown cold

God's gonna trouble the water

Heal my body, heal my soul

God's gonna trouble the water

Afraid

But I must go on

My flesh warring against me

The enemy trying to keep me bound

Still lying to me

In my ear

Saying

Don't bother

You will never succeed

No one can love you

Not even God

You

Want wholeness

There is none

And even if there was

You

Surely don't deserve it

Satan tightening the chains

Throwing loved ones in my path

Playing with my emotions

Cynthia Haynes

Trials and trials

Tribulation and tribulation

Everything spinning out of control

All things left behind

I can only move forward

Sorrow

Loathing

Anger

Hurt

Pain

Jealousy

Want me to stay

Crying

All the lies I've heard

Ringing in my ears

Tired

Weary

I must go on

God's gonna make me whole

I will crawl

To get there

Umm

How I yearn to be free

To be whole

Renewed

Restored

Delivered

My soul cries

Yes

My spirit screams

Freedom

I can see it

I can see the water

Satan trying harder

To keep me imprisoned

Life

The world

Emotions

Have held me captive

Far too long

Used people dear to me

Against me

Wounding my heart

Afflictions

Afflictions

And more afflictions

Satan

Wanting to steal my soul

Running

For each stumbling block

Every

Insecurity

Each tear

I run faster

And faster

Every lie the enemy ever told me

Any addictions

Hurt

Pain

Hate

Unforgiveness

Faster and faster

I run

My body is tired

But my spirit leads me

I'm almost there

I wanna look back

I can only go forward

My life

My past

Flashing before my eyes

I made it

The enemy has tried to slay me

Since I was a child

Cynthia Haynes

But I made it

Used loved ones against me

But I made it

Into the water

Each step

More empowering than the next

My spirit rejoices

Joy

Peace

Happiness

Runs through me

God troubled the water

He has restored my soul

Thank you, Jesus

I've been made whole

My soul cries

Yes

My spirit screams

Freedom

Freedom

I've been made whole

I'm whole

I'm whole

Thank you for the water

Thank you for the water, Jesus

Thank you for the water

Thank you for the water, Jesus!

1 Peter 3:17 NKJV

"For it is better, if it is the will of God, to suffer for doing good than for doing evil."

This Too Shall Pass

I could see it

It was there

I could almost touch it

Then the attacks came

One by one

They came

But I believed and I prayed

I believed and I prayed

I believed and I prayed

Then more attacks came

And I stood

I stood on my faith

On His word

More trials came

More and more

More and more they came

But I believed and I prayed

I believed and I prayed

I believed and I prayed

Then the enemy attacked my finances

But I stood

I stood on my faith

Because I know my ways aren't my Daddy's ways

Then came the stumbling blocks

Temptation

An easy way

But I resisted the enemy and he fled

I spoke victory—I spoke breakthroughs

I spoke prosperity

Then he came again

Cynthia Haynes

This time attacking my mind

Speaking to me

Speaking to me through others

But I spoke back

I am more than a conqueror

My Daddy did not bring me this far to leave me

I stood firm

I believed and I prayed

I believed and I prayed

I believed and I prayed

Then came the storm

And I praised Him and I thanked Him

I praised Him and I thanked Him

I praised Him and I thanked Him

Wondering how I would eat

How I would feed my children

And He made a way

He made a way out of no way

And we ate

Then the enemy attacked my heart

But I lifted up my Father

And I praised Him

The attacks starting coming full force

The enemy attacked my faith

The very faith I have been standing on

My flesh trying to overthrow my spirit

Placing doubt before my very eyes

At a crossroad

Which way to go

Left

Right

Forward

Backwards

Be still He whispers to me

And know that I AM

I AM THE GOD of Abraham, Isaac and Jacob

I AM

I am your Shepherd

Cynthia Haynes

You shall not want
I am with you
I know you are tired
But I will give you rest
I see the trials
I see what you are going through
But I am molding you
I am creating a faith warrior
Will you trust me, child?
Will you stand?
If I don't do what you know I can do
Will you still love Me?
Will you follow Me?
If you have no home
Will you still love Me?
Believe in Me?
Will you stand on your faith?
If you don't feel My presence
Will you still love Me?

Will you praise Me?

If you lose everything you hold dear?

Will you love Me?

Will you still say, "Yes, Lord"?

I'll love you

Remember, tribulation will come

But it is better to suffer for good than evildoings

That the trials will come and continue to come

But keep standing

For I am with you ALWAYS

Even when you can't see through

The hurt

Through the pain

Through the storm

I AM WITH YOU

And know that this too shall pass

THIS TOO SHALL PASS

John 7:38 NKJV

"He who believes in Me, as the Scripture has said, out of his heart will flow rivers of living water."

Flowin' with God

Each one of us has a unique flow with God

Called according to His will and His purpose

I write

God flows

I write

God flows

I write

God flows

His words flow through me

Spitting out of my hands like fire

Bringing

Revelation

Healing

Deliverance

A word for the lost

I write

God flows

I write

God flows

I write

God flows

As my hands begin to write

To His melody

He speaks, I write

Simultaneously we are in sync

Like the steady beating of a heart

Bump, bump, bump, bump, bump, bump, bump

I write, God flows

I write, God flows

I write

Cynthia Haynes

God flows

We flow together like

The dancing of trees

To the warm summer breeze

Swaying from side to side

Side to side

In perfect harmony

I write, God flows

He flows through me like the rushing of a current

Bringing

Serenity

Peace

Encouragement

Liberty

I write and God flows

His words come like a bolt of lightning

Surging through my entire being

Flowing from my hand

As my pen hits the paper

He speaks, I write

He speaks, I write

He speaks

I write

I am his vessel

He flows through me in poetic form

He speaks

His will

I write

His vessel

He speaks

His will

I write

His vessel

He speaks

His will

I write

His vessel

Each word that flows through me

Cynthia Haynes

Coming from the spirit of God

Is like thunder

Shaking everything to its core

Making the devil tremble

I write

God flows

God flows

I write

I write

God flows

The enemy fears me because he knows

With God flowing through me, I become one with God

That there is

Wholeness

Repentance

Abundance

I write

God flows

I'm free

I write

God flows

I'm free

I write

God flows

I'm free

His words overtake me like a whirlwind

Pouring into my soul

His comfort

Hope

Love

He is the potter

And I the clay

He has molded me to use me

I write, God flows

I write, God flows

I write

God flows

I am His instrument—His pupil

Cynthia Haynes

Waiting for His instruction

Taking no thought for what I write

Writing as it is being spoken

His flow breaks yokes

Cancels assignments

And sets captives free

I write, God flows

He speaks, I write

God

Flows

The enemy has tried to kill and stop me

Because he knew once I walked into my destiny

That there was no stopping God's plan for my life

Eye has not seen

Ear has not heard

Neither has it entered into the heart of man

What God has prepared for me

I write, God flows

I write, God flows

I write

God flows

Many are called

And few are chosen

I didn't choose God

He chose me before the foundation of this world

Before I was even in my mother's belly, He knew me

He has ordained, anointed and appointed me

I am His poetic messenger

His scribe

I have a scribal anointing

I write, God flows

I write, God flows

Marriages restored

I write, God flows

I write, God flows

Souls are saved

I write, God flows

I write, God flows

Cynthia Haynes

Purpose is revealed

I write. God flows

I write, God flows

The bound are made free

I write, God flows

I write, God flows

Generational curses destroyed

God flows, I write

God flows, I write

Bitterness replaced with Peace

God flows, I write

God flows, I write

Hurt replaced with Joy

God flows, I write

God flows, I write

Pain replaced with Happiness

God flows, I write

God flows, I write

Hate replaced with Love

He speaks, I write and God flows

His words create the flow

His flow is the poem

There is no poem without His flow

So

I write and God flows

I write, God flows

I write

God flows

2 Corinthians 5:17 NKJV

"Therefore, if anyone is in Christ, he is a new creation; old things have passed away; behold, all things have become new."

Don't get it Twisted (I Know Who I Am)

I know who I was

Where I've been

What I've done

What I was

I was a sinner

Lost, blind

Dumb and confused

The path I had chosen was leading me to hell

I've done many things I am not proud of

The enemy has constantly reminded me of my past

And things I've done

My life was an emotional roller coaster

Then one day I got saved

I accepted Christ

As my Lord and Savior

John 14:6 says

"I am the way, the truth, and the life; no man comes to the father but by me"

So I tried walking the straight and narrow path

And I fell and got up

I'd fall and I'd get up

I'd fall and I'd get up

And sometimes I'd fall

And it would take me a really long time to get up

See, someone once told me that

Sin takes you further than you wanted to go

Makes you stay longer than you wanted to stay

And makes you pay more than you wanted to pay

Cynthia Haynes

I know

I lived that life

I have gone astray

I've walked away

And I wouldn't even pray

I was too ashamed to pray

To ask forgiveness

I liked where I was

I was fooled, deceived, hood winked and bamboozled

By the enemy

But God loved me so much

That He came and got me

He'll leave ninety nine sheep just to bring that one lost sheep home

It's not His will that anyone should perish

But have everlasting life

He's married to the backslider

I was that backslider

And even though I backslid

He came and got ME

I was lost, but now I'm found

Don't get it twisted

I know who I was

I know who I am

Till this day

The enemy whispers to me

Trying to remind me of who I was, who I've hurt, what I was

Throwing things in my face

Using the same tactics

Trying to keep me bound

But who the Son sets free is free indeed

I know I'm free

I am a sinner saved by Grace

I know who I was

I wanted to fit in

I wanted acceptance

Had low self esteem

Cynthia Haynes

Yearned for somebody to love me

So I walked away

Time and time again

I walked away

I wouldn't pray

I was too caught up in me

What I wanted to do

I was caught up in my flesh

My will, not my Father's

So I started playing church

Acting like I was holy, sanctified and filled with the Holy Ghost

So people would like me

Then I'd go home and smoke a cigarette

Listen to my worldly music

Start cursing

Representing a false god

One that I created

A god that would fit my needs and accommodate my lifestyle

Then one day I got tired

Tired of running in circles, circles and more circles

Trying to find happiness

In all the wrong places

Trying to get joy from the world

Even though inside

My spirit knew

True joy comes from God

One day I met the enemy

I remember that day like it was yesterday

On my birthday

I was still in a rebellious state

Not wanting to come back

I liked where I was

I was comfortable there

But God was calling me back

I couldn't run anymore

I couldn't run from His voice

His call

Cynthia Haynes

That day I heard His voice

I hardened not my heart

I fell on my knees and I cried

It was a great cry

Begging for forgiveness

Repenting for the wrong I've done

I rededicated my life

He spoke to me and told me on this day I would be celebrating my rebirth

That the angels were rejoicing

I laid it at the cross

So from that day forward

I picked up my cross and I walked

I picked up my cross and I walked

I picked up my cross and I walked

As heavy as it was

I picked up my cross and I walked

There were many trials, much tribulation, many stumbling blocks

The enemy started using loved ones against me

I even wrote a poem about it

God's gonna trouble the water

That was another turning point

No more could I let the enemy

Use loved ones against me

I'd have to pray for them

But how can I pray for others when I don't even pray for myself?

I decided no more

That's another poem

To touch the hem of His garment

Where I told Satan he couldn't have me anymore

See all the things that I went through

I realize now

They were of my own doing

Some were tests, trials, attacks and God was molding me

All things work together for good to them that love God

I learned to stop questioning God

And stop asking why

I won't always understand why things happen

But I know it's all a part of His divine plan

Don't get it twisted; I know who I was and I know who I am

See, I used to be a perpetrator—a manipulator

Did what pleased self

That's who I was

Not who I am

The day I accepted Jesus

The day I gave my life

I gained my life

The day I let go and let God

And started walking in his will

Is the day that I was reborn?

Was the day I could truly see?

I was blind, but now I see

I see

I see that the path I was walking was leading me straight to hell

I see that God's grace and his mercy is sufficient

That His love is everlasting

I see the error of my ways

I see my sins had me bound

Held me captive

I see the tactics the enemy uses to try and get me back

Don't get it twisted

I know who I was

I know who I am

Although my sins are like scarlet, they shall be white as snow

Though they are red like crimson, they shall be as wool

Who I was

I'm not her anymore

See, I used to write poetry

Thinking it was for me

So I kept it to myself

Once I started sharing it

With people and I felt accepted

I started to serve self

Cynthia Haynes

Read it for self gratification

Not to give God the Glory

Now when I write

I don't write for me

Sometimes I wouldn't write

Because the poems sounded the same

Repetitious even

But I see I don't write for me; I write for God

I flow for Christ

Knowing obedience is better

Than sacrifice

Don't get it twisted; I know who I am

I am

A child of God

I am more than a conqueror

I am fearfully and wonderfully made

I am a princess

Because I am an heir of my Father

I know I can do all things through Christ who

strengthens me

I am blessed

Highly favored

And walking in the righteousness of God

I am a woman of God

A servant of the Most High

Great works will I do

I know who I am

I am a soldier

A warrior

And nothing can separate me from the love of God

He reigns

Don't get it twisted

I am a child

Of the King

www.ingramcontent.com/pod-product-compliance
Lightning Source LLC
Chambersburg PA
CBHW021133300426
44113CB00006B/410